BRAIN POWER

TEST◇YOUR
INTELLIGENCE

BRAIN POWER

NORMAN SULLIVAN

WARD LOCK

A WARD LOCK BOOK

First published in the UK
1993 by Ward Lock
(a Cassell imprint)
Villiers House
41/47 Strand
London
WC2N 5JE

Distributed in the United States
by Sterling Publishing Co., Inc.
387 Park Avenue South, New York, NY 10016-8810

Distributed in Australia
by Capricorn Link (Australia) Pty Ltd
P.O. Box 665, Lane Cove, NSW 2066

British Library Cataloguing-in-Publication Data
A catalogue record for this book is available from the British Library

ISBN 0 7063 7130 5

Printed and bound in Great Britain by
Cox & Wyman Ltd, Reading, Berks

Contents

Read This First 6

Read This First

When a person suffers a simple fracture of an arm or a leg, Nature comes to the rescue and provides its own 'glue', which, in six weeks or so, joins the broken bone so that the patient is considered fit to undergo physiotherapy. No time is lost before starting this course of treatment because several weeks of enforced inertia will cause the limb to become 'lazy' through lack of use, and the muscles will become flaccid. Only a carefully devised programme of exercises can ensure recovery, after which, with the limb mended and the muscles strengthened, the patient is as good as new and able to carry on a normal life.

Although physiotherapy after an accident is endured philosophically in the knowledge that it is essential for recovery, many people recognize the value of physical exercise and enjoy it for its own sake, in whatever form it takes – jogging, swimming, sport or even walking – as a way of keeping fit and remaining in good health.

Few would deny that there is much benefit to be derived from physical exercise, and many go to great lengths in their quest to keep fit. As long as the exercise is not overdone and is kept within the limitations of the participant, especially with regard to age, it can only redound to that person's good. It can strengthen the limbs and muscles, improve the figure, tone up the body and generally create a sense of well-being.

If physical exercise is beneficial to the body, is it a fanciful notion that mental exercise is beneficial to the brain?

Your brain is constantly in action (even when you are asleep), although for most of the time you may not be putting it to any excessive use, allowing it to wander free, as it were, in its own way and in its own time. However, when it is concentrating hard on one specific task, your brain moves into 'top gear'. It is like a car engine 'ticking over' when receiving no impetus or speeding up when it is called on to use its full capacity. The extent to which it is brought into action or the frequency with which it has to offer its full potential depends on you, the 'driver'. Some people are content to stay in the slow lane all the time, while others are eager to take the fast lane and reach their destination as quickly as possible.

Just as many people cannot be bothered to indulge in physical exercise, so there are many people who regard settling down with a crossword puzzle or any type of puzzle or game that relies on what Hercule Poirot would have called 'those little grey cells' a waste of time. Sometimes this prejudice against 'intellectual' pastimes is because there is no inclination and not because of any lack of ability; such pursuits simply have no appeal. But judging from the enormous numbers that follow radio and television panel games and quizzes and the fact that new ones are constantly being devised, it would seem that many people do enjoy programmes that tax their brains. Even newspapers are increasingly publishing daily puzzles and quizzes in addition to the ubiquitous crossword puzzles.

On the other hand, many people take pride in accepting a mental challenge. They cannot bear the idea of doing nothing, and spend their leisure time doing crossword or jigsaw puzzles, reading, writing or playing patience – anything, in fact, as long as they are mentally occupied. Others follow a hobby of their choice, but with the same objective – they want to be doing something, rather than idling.

Although it is a wonderful invention and a boon to people who live alone, television is, in many ways, a drawback, killing off many pleasant aspects of social life and putting a stop to conversation. Apart from the very limited amount of concentration that most programmes of a 'quiz' nature demand, it deprives the brain of exercise of any value.

The value of a healthy mind in a healthy body was extolled nearly two thousand years ago by Juvenal: *Orandum est ut sit mens sana in corpore sano* ('Your prayer must be for a sound mind in a sound body'). Researchers at Manchester University in the UK have recently conducted a study of nearly 8,000 people, which showed that physically fit older people retain the mental skills of many who are 35 years younger. Experiments using intelligence tests, carried out for up to 10 years on men and women aged between 50 and 96, established a firm link between health and mental ability. An intelligent person has more brain cells, and a psychologist in Yorkshire claims that even under the influence of heavy drinking, an intelligent person loses fewer of these cells than a person of low mentality and with no qualifications. An American scientist has claimed that a course of certain vitamin tablets increased students' IQs by one or two points (although this claim has been dismissed by British courts).

If these discoveries and theories are to be believed it appears that there is a direct link between good health and intellect and that mental ability is likely to be improved – or at least kept 'up to scratch' – by keeping the body fit and healthy.

Exercising the brain on problems designed to stimulate intense concentration improves the ability to cope with other problems in the future. 'Intelligence' may be related to one's ability to grapple successfully with problems, even when there is no affinity with the subject. Solving problems that at first appear insoluble may be a matter of recognizing a logical starting-point and putting oneself in the position of the problem-setter. The person setting the problem must have had something in mind that could lead to the solution, otherwise there would be no validity in the problem. At the same time – and especially in the case of more difficult problems – the solution must not be so obvious that it could be seen at a glance. 'Distractors' – alternative lines of approach – must be such that the solver has to choose between the obvious and the less obvious.

In this connection Edward de Bono, the British psychologist and author of the book *Lateral Thinking*, has defined a method of solving problems by using the imagination as opposed to the more obvious step-by-step approach. Indeed, the very words 'lateral thinking' have fallen into common usage today. A simple and elementary problem may be solved by straightforward logical reasoning, such as in the example: 'What letter comes next – O C T O B E – ? ' As there is no other word than October that starts in this way, there can be no alternative answer.

But more complex problems may demand more complex reasoning, as in this example: 'What time is shown at X?'

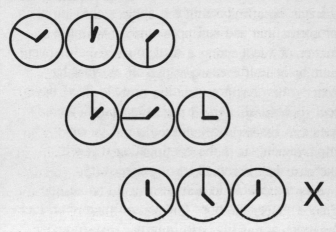

At first sight it would appear that the clocks are arranged haphazardly. Yet, if the problem is fair, there must be some relationship between them. It is natural to consider them in the order in which they are arranged, but as no clue is offered by this method, another approach must be chosen. If they are considered *alternately*, starting from the second clock, it is obvious that they advance the time in a regular sequence: 1 o'clock, 2 o'clock, 3 o'clock and then 4 o'clock. So X must be 5 o'clock. The alternate clocks starting from the first *are* arranged haphazardly, merely as distractors from the correct solution. Had the distractors been omitted, the answer would have been obvious, and the problem, instead of being fairly difficult, would have been easy.

Even though you might grapple with a problem for some time and still not come up with the answer, the fact remains that you will have given your brain useful exercise, which, if what has been written has any validity, must in itself have been beneficial. Early exercise in physiotherapy does not always show immediate signs of improvement; it is the continuation of such exercise that eventually brings recovery.

It is reasonable to assume that the more one plays a game that does not depend merely on luck the more one is likely to improve at it. In active sports, if improvement comes with practice it generally continues until a peak in performance is achieved and until a certain age is reached, after which a decline – both physical (as limbs become less agile) and mental (as reactions become slower) – sets in.

The same applies to mental activity, except that the age at which ability peaks is considerably greater than in physical activity and the decline sets in much later. The more the brain is used the more likely it is to improve, and intelligence grows more readily in fertile soil that is constantly being tended than in barren soil that is neglected. There are, therefore, advantages to be gained from trying to solve the problems in this book, even if you are unsuccessful. They are that the problems will be a test of your intelligence as it is at the present time; they may improve your intelligence so that you will fare better in later tests of a similar nature; but, more importantly, they are exercising your brain.

The question remains, however: what sort of tests should be included in such a book? To give a test on one subject would demonstrate the 'brain power' (or lack of it) in that subject but would hardly be evidence of 'intelligence', if that word means, as has been suggested, the ability to grapple successfully with problems even if there is no affinity with the subject. For this reason a fairly balanced selection of various subjects is offered, and a person who scores well in one subject may fare badly in another. Thus, a more realistic appraisal of intelligence can be obtained from a cross-section of a diversity of subjects.

A person of normal intelligence should at least attempt to solve a problem in a subject with which there is no familiarity, and in pre-testing the questions in this book an average rating of almost exactly 40 per cent was achieved.

Although the book lays no claim to labelling you with an IQ factor, if you achieve a factor of 40 per cent you will know that you are of at least 'average' intelligence. An overall rating of more than 40 per cent would indicate that your intelligence (within the definition of that word) is better than average, and I leave it to you how you choose to quantify it on the basis of 40 per cent representing a normal IQ of 100, although I would prefer that you did not take your results too seriously.

The subjects covered in this book are: *verbal understanding*, including a knowledge of basic spelling and the meaning of words; *numerical skill*, either in written or mental calculation, the only condition being that you do not use a pocket calculator; *visuo-spatial discrimination*, which is the ability to recognize shapes and patterns, especially when their positions are changed relative to the viewer; *visual perception*, including the matching of similar patterns, the only condition being that you do not use tracing paper; *knowledge*, although only a very small number of problems rely on knowledge, which in itself bears little relationship to intelligence, even though it is fair to assume that an 'intelligent' person would be *au fait* with topical subjects and widely known events; and *deduction*, which plays a prominent part in many of the problems, whether they are classified as verbal, spatial or numerical, for they may also call for deduction – that is, inferring what the problem-setter had in mind in arranging the component parts of the problem.

Although it is understandable that there may be a temptation to browse through the pages that follow before beginning to concentrate seriously, do not linger over any question that catches your eye at this stage.

When you decide to start working seriously on the tests, begin by equipping yourself with writing materials; not only do a few of the problems involve a limited amount of writing – although the majority can be answered simply with a letter or number – but you must also keep a note of your scores in each test so that you can find out how you rate at the end. You should also note the time you start each test. In schoolroom conditions you would be requested to cease work as soon as the time allowed had expired, and you will find these tests more meaningful if you do them under 'classroom conditions'.

There are 15 problems in each test. If each problem took only one minute, the whole test would take 15 minutes, but some questions are much more difficult than others, and the time limits take full account of this.

Never give up too readily on any one problem if the answer does not strike you right away. Some of the questions are deliberately designed to make you exercise your brain to the full, and the time limits allow adequate extra time when necessary.

The time limits which you will see at the beginning of each test, take the following factors into consideration:

- some people write more slowly than others, and the time allows for slow rather than quick writers;
- a few problems call for some basic drawing, although most answers require only a letter or number;
- some problems involve more writing than others (regardless of the speed of writing), although in no case is much writing necessary;
- the relative difficulty of each problem.

Some of you may consider that the time limits are too generous; others may not be able to answer all the questions in the time allowed. This in itself points to a difference in mental ability, since speed of appraisal is also a mark of intelligence. After all, the answer to most problems would come eventually if there were time.

You should note the time you start each test and finish working on it as soon as the time limit is reached. By all means continue to work on the remaining problems, but do not include the answers in your score. You will find the scores on the pages following the tests, together with explanations of the answers. Keep a note of your score in each test until you reach the end of the book.

Should you score full marks in any one test, you may award yourself one bonus point in addition to the marks you have scored.

Altogether there are 11 tests. These are graduated so that those in Group I are easy, those in Group II are more difficult, and those in Group III are difficult. Although ideally each test should be taken in one sitting and in a quiet environment, you may, for whatever reasons, have to fit them in when you have spare moments. Dealing with them in a piecemeal way does not matter, as long as you are careful to time each period that you can devote to the test.

Do not skip from one unfinished test to another, but undertake each one separately, making sure that you understand the explanations of the answers of problems you failed to solve before proceeding to the next test.

The best way to go about any one test is to read quickly through it and decide which problems appeal to your own particular strengths. If numeracy is your strong point you will probably pick problems of that kind; if you are strong on words you will probably pick the verbal problems. Begin by answering the questions that are easy for you. This will give you maximum time to spend on what you consider to be the difficult problems until either the time runs out or you solve them all. Spending too long on a problem that stumps you could waste valuable time, during which you might score several points on other problems.

In conclusion, and despite the advice I have offered regarding scoring, ratings, method of approach and so forth, I fully realize that many readers will prefer merely to treat this book as an ordinary 'puzzle book' and work their way through the tests haphazardly, with no regard for scoring or timing.

It is up to you. After all, the book is primarily intended to give pleasure and entertainment – and, of course, to exercise your brain and provide plenty of mental therapy. If solving the problems exercises your brain half as much as devising them exercised mine, only good can result.

So I end by wishing you 'Good (mental) health!'

Norman Sullivan

GROUP I
– Easy –

Time limit: 20 minutes

1. Which is the odd one out?

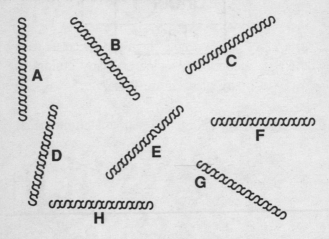

2. Counting down, first by one place, then by two places, then by three and so on (adding one extra place each time), as in this example – 15, 14, 12, 9, 5, 0 – which of these numbers will finish at zero?

102   103   104   105   106

3. What will go in front of all these to make complete words?

_ _ _ _ _ _ _NOMY
_ _ _ _ _ _ _GRAPH
_ _ _ _ _ _ _PSY

4. How many triangles are there here?

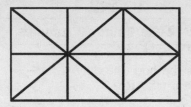

5. In a party of 35 people there are twice as many women as children and twice as many children as men. How many of each are there?

6. Arrange these cubes into four matching pairs:

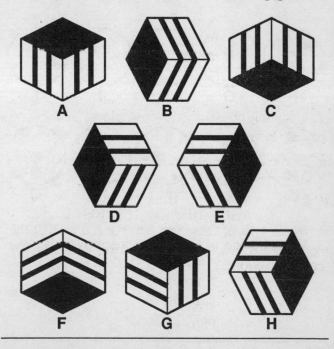

7. Which is the odd one out?
   A. BACKGAMMON
   B. PAGAN
   C. INUNDATED
   D. SEVERAL
   E. UNPOPULAR

8. Which is the odd one out?

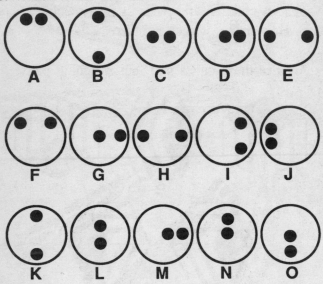

9. Which **two** of these can be reversed so that the total of each row – across and down – equals 10?

A. 5 4 1
B. 6 1 3
C. 3 5 2

10. What goes into the empty brackets?

```
 1  2 (2 8 4 6) 3  4
 4  5 (1 2 2 1 1 5 1 8) 6  7
 7  8 (2 8 4 0 3 2 3 6) 9 10
11 12 (                 ) 13 14
```

11. Which is the odd one out?

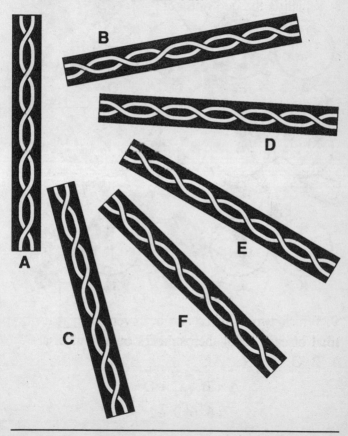

12. Which of the figures at the bottom – A, B, C or D – follows number 4?

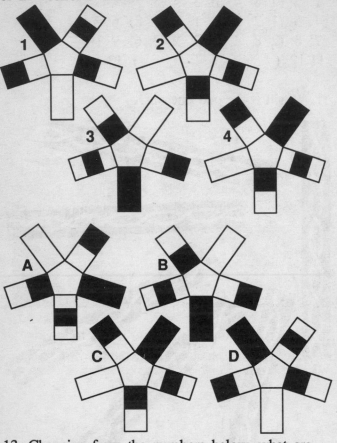

13. Choosing from the numbers below, what are A, B, C and D?

$$A \times B + C \div D = 5$$

6 6 9 12

14. Which of the following statements are true and which are false?

A. If this clock is gaining, the pendulum weight should be moved downwards.

B. The majority of these shapes are convex.

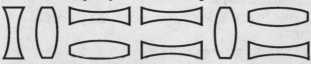

C. A spider has six legs.

D. The majority of these are stalagmites.

15. What is the sum of numbers in the following list which are consecutive (for example 3, 4, 5)?

15	5	10	28
24	7	18	26
11	21	17	13
22	9	1	20

NOW CHECK YOUR ANSWERS
AND KEEP A NOTE OF YOUR SCORE.

Answers

1. E (Score 1 point)

The designs consist of the letter S repeated 10 times, but in E one of them is the wrong way round.

2. 105 (Score 1 point)

3. AUTO (Score 1 point)

The words are AUTONOMY, AUTOGRAPH and AUTOPSY.

4. 25 (Score 1 point)

5. 5 men, 10 children and 20 women (**Score 1 point if all correct**)

If x = the number of men, then x + 2x + 4x = 35

therefore 7x = 35

so x = 5

6. A-C, B-F, D-G, E-H (Score 1 point if all correct)

7. A (Score 1 point)

All the others contain palindromes (words that read the same forwards and backwards). B. pAGAn, C. iNUNdated, D. sEVEral, E. unPOPular.

8. G (Score 1 point)

All the others can be paired: A–J, B–E, C–L, D–N, F–I, H–K and M–O.

9. B and C (Score 1 point)
They become: 5 4 1
3 1 6
2 5 3

10. 55706065 (Score 1 point)

In the first line multiply the digits outside the brackets by 2 in this order: extreme left, extreme right, second left and first right. In the second line multiply by 3 and in the third line by 4, following the same procedure. Therefore, in the fourth line multiply by 5 and follow the same procedure.

11. B (Score 1 point)

The two strands should pass over and under each other alternately, as in the other examples.

12. D (Score 1 point)

They all rotate clockwise, first to the next vane, then missing one, then two and so on.

13. A is 9 or 6, B is 6 or 9, C is 6, D is 12 **(Score 1 point if all correct)**

$9 \times 6 + 6 \div 12 = 5$

14. **(Score 1 point if all correct)** A is true; B is false (the majority are concave); C is false (a spider has eight legs); D is false (a stalagmite grows upwards, whereas a stalactite grows downwards).

15. 128 (Score 1 point)

The consecutive numbers are: 9, 10, 11; 17, 18; 20, 21 and 22.

REMEMBER TO KEEP A NOTE OF YOUR SCORE.

Notes: To start you off in an easy way, there were no great difficulties here. In Question 4 you may have under-estimated the number of triangles, and Question 10 may have held you up and caused problems in view of the time limit imposed.

Test 2

1. What comes next in this series?

   1 7 8 15 23 38 61 –

2. Which is the odd one out?

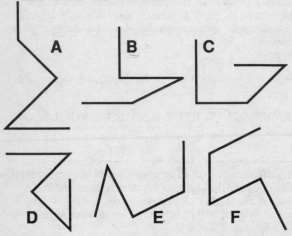

3. What word is this? (Clue: 'It's in the news.')

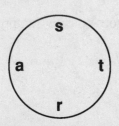

4. Which piece completes the letter H?

5. Which, if any, of these words are spelt wrongly?

- A. AGRESSIVE
- B. COMMUNICATION
- C. HAMPSTER
- D. DECEIVED
- E. CIELING
- F. SEIGE
- G. GRANDEUR
- H. NECCESARY
- I. AQUAINTANCE
- J. ACCESORY

6. What number goes into the empty brackets?

```
  9 8 (7 9) 1 2 6
1 0 5 (7 9) 1 3 5
  4 8 (3 5) 8 0
  3 4 (   ) 8 5
```

7.

If  is **LEAK**

what is ?

8. What words are indicated here?

   A. 1 4 2 8 9
   B. 6 1 5 3 11 60 20

9.

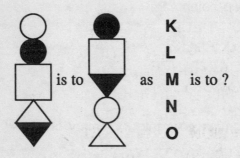 is to   as

K
L
M is to ?
N
O

10. What is X?

    25 22 15 X   10 19 24

11. What are X and Y?

    72 7 36 14 18 28 9 56 X Y

12. Which is the odd one out?

    A. 1   6   3   4   9   2
    B. 6 14   3   8   1   2
    C. 19   7   5 23   3   4
    D. 1   9   4   7   3   2

13. Pair the words in the first column with words in the second column:

    A. FOOT   1. TAKING
    B. GOAL   2. LANGUAGE
    C. WICKET   3. NET
    D. DOOR   4. BALL
    E. SIGN   5. KEEPER
    F. FOREIGN   6. MARKET
    G. STOCK   7. POST
    H. RACING   8. MAN
    I. FREE   9. EXCHANGE
    J. FISH   10. CAR

14. What are A, B and C?

3	A	6
C	4	B
B	2	B	A

15. What is X?

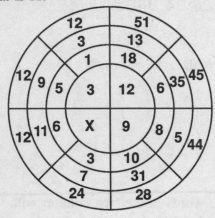

NOW CHECK YOUR ANSWERS
AND KEEP A NOTE OF YOUR SCORE.

Answers

1. 99 (Score 1 point)

After the first two terms each subsequent term is the sum of the two previous terms.

2. D (Score 1 point)

All the others contain one acute angle, one obtuse angle and one right angle. D contains two acute angles and no obtuse angle.

3. STAR (Score 1 point)

S is north (N); T is east (E); A is west (W) and R is south (S).

4. D (Score 1 point)

It fits like this:

5. A, C, E, F, H, I and J (Score 1 point if all correct)

AGGRESSIVE, HAMSTER, CEILING, SIEGE, NECESSARY, ACQUAINTANCE and ACCESSORY.

6. 25 (Score 1 point)

In the first row divide the numbers outside the brackets by 14 and put the results inside the brackets. Continue in the same way, but next dividing by 15 and then by 16. In the last row divide by 17.

7. HIGH (Score 1 point)

The minute hands indicate the first and third letters – 8 is H, the eighth letter; 7 is G, the seventh letter. The hour hands indicate the second and fourth letters – 9 is I, the ninth letter; 8 is H, the eighth letter.

8. A - OFTEN, B - SOFTEST (Score 1 point if both correct)

The letters are the initials of the numbers: One Four Two Eight Nine and Six One Five Three Eleven Sixty Twenty.

9. L M O K N (arranged vertically) **(Score 1 point)**

Transpose the letters in the same order as the figures.

10. 4 **(Score 1 point)**

The first term is followed by the last term; the second term is followed by the penultimate term, and the third term follows the same procedure. Thus the series becomes: 25 24 22 19 15 10 4(X) – ie, decreasing by one more each time: -1 -2 -3 -4 -5 -6(X).

11. X is $4\frac{1}{2}$ or 4.5, Y is 112 **(Score 1 point if both correct)**

Halve the terms alternately from the first term: 72 36 18 9 $4\frac{1}{2}$ or 4.5 (X). Double the terms alternately from the second term: 7 14 28 56 112(Y).

12. D **(Score 1 point)**

Add the numbers and then add the remaining digits: A – total of numbers is 25, 2 plus 5 = 7; B – total of numbers is 34, 3 plus 4 = 7; C – total of numbers is 61, 6 plus 1 = 7; D – total of numbers is 26, 2 plus 6 = 8.

13. A–4, B–7, C–5, D–8, E–2, F–9, G–1, H–10, I–6, J–3 **(Score 1 point if all correct)**

14. A is 7, B is 1, C is 8 **(Score 1 point if all correct)**

With a four-figure total, the calculation is obviously addition and not subtraction. In order to reconcile the units with the tens, B must be 1 (the units total 7), so that 7 added to 4 in the tens gives 11, confirming that B is 1 (also confirmed in the final total). To give 2 in the final total, C must be 8, so that the hundreds come to 12.

15. $4\frac{1}{2}$ or 4.5 **(Score 1 point)**

In each quarter halve each total of the rings up to and including the centre. Thus, in the bottom left quarter: 24 plus 12 = 36, 11 plus 7 =18, 6 plus 3 = 9. Therefore X = $4\frac{1}{2}$ or 4.5.

REMEMBER TO KEEP A NOTE OF YOUR SCORE.

Notes: Spelling does not claim a high priority in modern education, and points were lost in Question 5. The last line in Question 6 may have led you to the fact that the numbers in that line are divisible by 17. Many people, failing (by lateral thinking) to reconcile letters with numbers, would have been caught out by Question 8.

Test 3

Time limit: 40 minutes

1. Which leaves obviously came from the same plant?

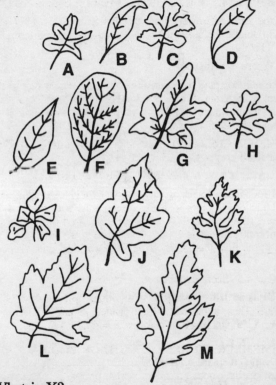

2. What is X?

   X   11   1098   76   5   43   21

3. Which letter in the first column belongs to the second column and which letter in the second column belongs to the first column?

A	B
H	C
I	D
M	E
O	F
R	G
T	J
U	K
V	L
W	N
X	P
	Q
	S
	Y
	Z

4. Which is the odd one out?

    A. UNCLEAN
    B. FINAL
    C. REASONABLE
    D. SMOTHERED
    E. DAUNTLESS

5. Which is the odd one out?

    A. SEARCHING
    B. ANARCHIST
    C. SCORCHING
    D. CHURCHMAN
    E. OVERCHARGE
    F. MARCHES

6. What are X, Y and Z?

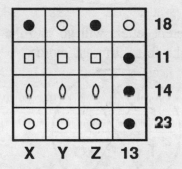

7. Among these dominoes how many double-sixes are there?

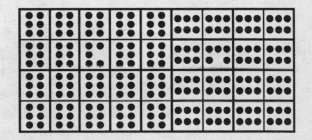

---

8. Which slice has been cut from the cake?

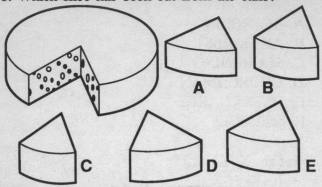

9. Four different letters will go into the empty space to make four different words.

10. What is the ratio between A and C?

A. 2 to 1
B. 4 to 1
C. 1 to 1
D. 5 to 1

11. Why are these dates relevant to this moment?

    A. 4th April
    B. 3rd January
    C. 6th August
    D. 2nd February
    E. 3rd July
    F. 5th April
    G. 4th April
    H. 3rd August
    I. 4th June
    J. 1st November
    K. 2nd October
    L. 2nd September

12. A card-player holds 13 cards of four suits, of which seven are black and six are red. There are twice as many hearts as clubs and twice as many diamonds as hearts. How many spades does he hold?

13. Which word will go inside the brackets to complete the other four words?

      D E ( ) D
   C O M ( ) D O
     H U ( ) I T Y
     R O ( ) T I C

14. What is X?

131   517   192   X

15. Arrange these into four matching pairs

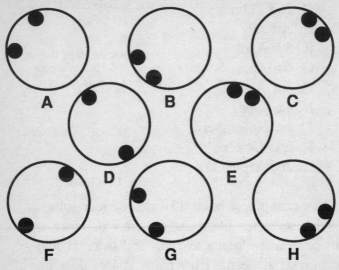

A   B   C

D   E

F   G   H

**NOW CHECK YOUR ANSWERS
AND KEEP A NOTE OF YOUR SCORE.**

Answers

1. C and H (Score 1 point)

2. 12 (Score 1 point)

The series must be read backwards and spaced correctly: 1 2 3 4 5 6 7 8 9 10 11 12(X).

3. R and Y (Score 1 point if both correct)

In the first column all the letters would look the same if reflected in a mirror, with the exception of R. In the second column all the letters would look different if reflected in a mirror, with the exception of Y.

4. B (Score 1 point)

All the others contain relations: A. UNCLEan, C. reaSONable, D. sMOTHERed, E. dAUNTless.

5. E (Score 1 point)

All the others contain RCH *in the centre* of the words: A. seaRCHing, B. anaRCHist, C. scoRCHing, D. chuRCHman, F. maRCHes. E – oveRCHarge – also contains these letters, but not in the centre.

6. X is 16, Y is 21, Z is 16 (Score 1 point if all correct)

To justify the right-hand vertical row with the top row, ● must be 2. Substituting this in the remaining horizontal rows, it becomes obvious that □ must be three, () must be 4 and, in the bottom row, ○ must be 7. The values for X, Y and Z now become clear.

7. 16 (Score 1 point)

The spots on two of the dominoes total 11, not 12.

8. E (Score 1 point)

9. H, P, T, V (Score 1 point if all correct)

The words are EXHORT, EXPORT, EXTORT and VORTEX.

10. A (Score 1 point)

Pinion A has 10 teeth. Pinion C has 20 teeth. Therefore the ratio between them is exactly 2 to 1, which is obtained by dividing the larger by the smaller. In other words, pinion A will make two revolutions while pinion C makes one. The number of teeth on the intermediate pinion does not in any way alter the ratio between the other two.

11. Because they spell INTELLIGENCE **(Score 1 point)**

A. April (4th letter)
B. January (3rd letter)
C. August (6th letter)
D. February (2nd letter)
E. July (3rd letter)
F. April (5th letter)

G. April (4th letter)
H. August (3rd letter)
I. June (4th letter)
J. November (1st letter)
K. October (2nd letter)
L September (2nd letter)

12. 6 **(Score 1 point)**

The player holds 1 club, 2 hearts and 4 diamonds. As he holds 13 cards (or seven black cards), it follows that there must be 6 spades.

13. MAN **(Score 1 point)**

The words are DEMAND, COMMANDO, HUMANITY and ROMANTIC.

14. 1 **(Score 1 point)**

Spaced correctly, the series becomes: 13 15 17 19 2(1).

15. A–G, B–H, C–E, D–F **(Score 1 point if all correct)**

REMEMBER TO KEEP A NOTE OF YOUR SCORE.

Notes: When you are dealing with spatial discrimination, it is usually possible to recognize shapes, even when their positions are changed relative to the viewer. However, in question 2 it was a matter of recognizing the spacing of numbers instead of shapes. In numerical problems that involve series of numbers you must be on the look-out for incorrect spacing, and the answer generally becomes obvious once the series is spaced correctly. The answer to this question was less apparent because the series had to be read backwards as well. In Question 9 it is possible that V eluded you, so that you were unable to complete the word VORTEX.

Test 4

Time limit: 40 minutes

1. Group these symbols into five sets of three.

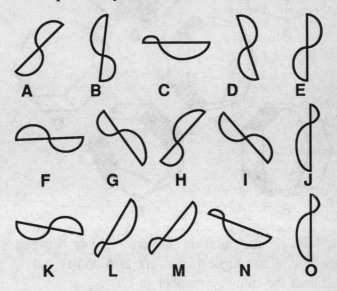

2. Which is the odd one out?

    A. DOCTOR
    B. TRUTH
    C. TAKINGS
    D. SUBTRACTS
    E. FLUKE

3. Group these six figures into three pairs.

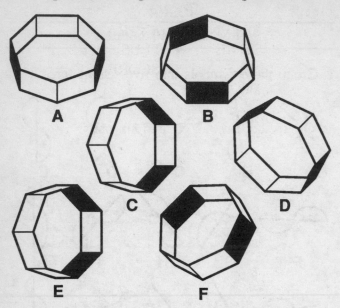

A B C D E F

4. Multiply the numbers that are midway between the lowest and highest numbers in A and B and subtract the midway number in C.

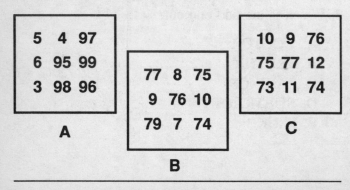

A
5 4 97
6 95 99
3 98 96

B
77 8 75
9 76 10
79 7 74

C
10 9 76
75 77 12
73 11 74

5. Arrange the following in ascending numerical order.

A. SEVEN   E. EXTRA
B. SOME   F. PLUS
C. NINE   G. SCORE
D. DOZEN

6. Group the illustrations into six pairs.

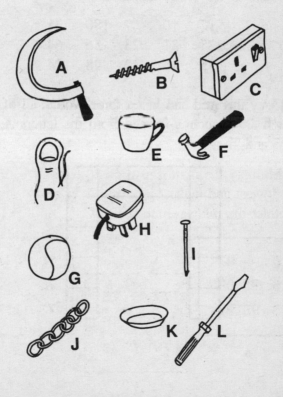

7. What goes into the empty square?

0	7	2	4	12	6	3
	7	9	6		18	9

8. Add the numbers that are squares of whole numbers to the prime numbers.

12	16	7	180	31
225	81	23	56	64
35	15	72	48	14

9. Copy this grid and insert three words, all of which are anagrams formed from the letters A, B, O, S and T.

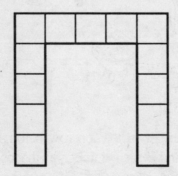

10. Which, if any, of these are wrong?

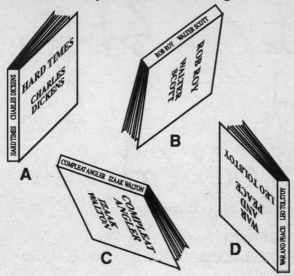

11. Which is the odd one out?

A. PEA
B. LOIN
C. SHORE
D. WALLOWS
E. TOGA
F. GARBED

12. Which number in the top row belongs to the bottom row, and which number in the bottom row belongs to the top row?

9	25	49	81	96
8	12	121	18	14

13. Which pair of spectacles is wrong?

14. Which is the odd one out?

A. TOMATO
B. TOBACCO
C. COCOA
D. OATMEAL
E. ALMOND
F. APPLE
G. LEMON

15. What are X and Y?

3	2
6	36

1	4
4	16

1	2
X	Y

**NOW CHECK YOUR ANSWERS
AND KEEP A NOTE OF YOUR SCORE.**

Answers

1. A–I–K, B–G–H, C–L–N, D–E–F, J–M–O (**Score 1 point if all correct**)

2. A (**Score 1 point**)

All the other words contain books in the Bible: B. tRUTH, C. taKINGS, D. subtrACTS and E. fLUKE.

3. A–D, B–F, C–E (**Score 1 point**)

4. 2,150 (**Score 1 point**)

51 is midway between 3 and 99; 43 is midway between 7 and 79; 51 x 43 = 2,193, less 43 (midway between 9 and 77) = 2,150.

5. C, A, E, F, G, D, B (**Score 1 point if all correct**)

NINE contains Roman numeral I = 1, SEVEN contains Roman numeral V = 5, EXTRA contains Roman numeral X = 10, PLUS contains Roman numeral L = 50, SCORE contains Roman numeral C = 100, DOZEN contains Roman numeral D – 500, SOME contains Roman numeral M =1000.

6. A-F, B-L, C-H, D-I, E-K, G-J (**Score 1 point if all correct**)

F (hammer) and A (sickle); B (screw) and L (screwdriver); C (socket) and H (plug); D (toe) and I (nail); E (cup) and K (saucer); G (ball) and J (chain).

7. 16 (**Score one point**)

Each number in the bottom row is the sum of the number above it and the previous number.

8. 447 (**Score one point**)

The square numbers are: 16 (4 squared), 225 (15 squared), 81 (9 squared) and 64 (8 squared), which equal 386. The prime numbers are: 7, 31 and 23, which equal 61. 386 + 61 = 447.

9. (Score 1 point)

B	O	A	T	S
O				A
A				B
S				O
T				T

10. A, B and C are wrong (**Score 1 point if all correct**)

The titles on the spines are printed the wrong way round. You can check by looking at the spine on this book! (The spine is that part of the cover that is visible when the book is placed on a shelf.)

11. D (**Score 1 point**)

This is an anagram of SWALLOW (a bird). The others are anagrams of animals; A. APE, B. LION, C. HORSE, E. GOAT and F. BADGER.

12. 96 and 121 (**Score 1 point if both correct**)

In the top row the numbers are square numbers (3, 5, 7, and 9) except 96; in the bottom row the numbers are even numbers (8, 12, 18 and 14) except 121 (which is the square of 11).

13. K (**Score 1 point**)

These spectacles should be bifocals, as in C and E

14. F (**Score 1 point**)

The other words each start with the last two letters of the previous word:

A. tomaTO
B. TObacCO
C. COcOA
D. OAtmeAL
E. ALmond
F. appLE
G. LEmon

15. X = 2, Y = 4 **(Score 1 point if both correct)**

The lower left-hand number is the product of the two top numbers; the bottom right-hand number is the square of the bottom left-hand number.

REMEMBER TO KEEP A NOTE OF YOUR SCORE.

Notes: If you started Question 6 by pairing F (the hammer) with I (the nail), you would have finished with A (the sickle) and D (the toe), which, of course, do not make a pair. You may have been caught out by Question 10. If the titles of books did not all run the same way, it would be extremely difficult to read them when they are placed side by side on a shelf.

NOW TOTAL YOUR SCORES FOR THE FIRST FOUR TESTS AND COMPARE THEM WITH THE RATINGS THAT FOLLOW.

Ratings in Group 1

Test 1 – average 7 points
Test 2 – average 5 points
Test 3 – average 7 points
Test 4 – average 7 points

Total for the group out of a possible 60 points

Over 51	Excellent
37 – 51	Very good
27 – 36	Good
26	Average
20 – 25	Fair
Under 20	Poor

If you scored under 20 you should go through the questions and answers again, especially those that you answered wrongly or failed to answer within the imposed time limits. Have you tackled tests of this nature before?

Try to get to grips with the reasoning behind the answers. You may find other problems which can be solved in a similar way, and the experience you have had with these should help you in the future tests.

Group II
– More Difficult –

Test 1

Time limit: 65 minutes
You may rest after 35 minutes and then
continue for another 30 minutes.

1. What is X?

   5   3   4   1   2   4   2   8   6   X

2. Which of the following statements are true and which are false?

    A. At 12.30 the hands of a clock form an
angle of 180 degrees.
    B. 15/16th is the same as 0.9375.
    C. The Andes are south of the Rockies.
    D. 15 capital letters of the alphabet consist
entirely of straight strokes.

3. Take the number that is midway between the highest and lowest numbers that are divisible by 13. Multiply this by the lowest even number, and subtract the highest odd number.

117	**8**	**63**	**43**
143	**12**	**97**	**39**
136	**27**	**91**	**3**

4. Which is the odd one out?

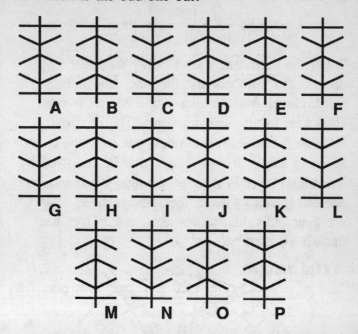

5. Change FOUR into NINE in six moves,
changing one letter at a time and making genuine
words each time.

```
     F  O  U  R
1.  _  _  _  _
2.  _  _  _  _
3.  _  _  _  _
4.  _  _  _  _
5.  _  _  _  _
6.  N  I  N  E
```

6. What is X?

1 7 8 14 X 30 20 6 14 7 8

7. On the dartboard shown below the outer ring doubles the numbers and the inner ring trebles them. Player A starts on a single 20 and moves clockwise in alternate segments. The next dart lands in a double, and the next one in a treble, and so on (a single, followed by a double, followed by a treble). Player B starts on a single 1 and moves alternately clockwise in the same manner. What are their individual scores after each player has thrown 10 darts?

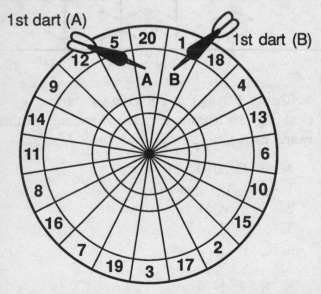

1st dart (A)

1st dart (B)

8. From this sign of the zodiac in code you should be able to decode the message from a boastful underground worker.

9. Write the singular or plural of each of these words as indicated in the brackets.

    A. GRAFFITI (singular)
    B. TYMPANUM (plural)
    C. CONCERTI (singular)
    D. TEMPO (plural)
    E. PHENOMENA (singular)
    F. CHARISMA (plural)
    G. LOCUS (plural)
    H. LIRA (plural)
    I. RADIUS (plural)

10. If TOM is 16 4 10 and DICK is 3 3 2 8, what is HARRY?

11. Which of the words below takes the place of X?

FAIRY = WOOF
BUBBLE = BESIDE
TABLE = X

BOW   CHAIR   COT   SOAP   SETTEE

12. Which is the odd one out?

13. Which of the numbers below takes the place of X?

7   3   9   7   12   X   16   18   21   25

5   6   8   12   14   15

14. Find words to fit the definitions. Each word is an anagram of the previous word but with one letter removed.

A. _ _ _ _ _ _ _ _ _ _ splashed
B. _ _ _ _ _ _ _ _ _ covered to excess
C. _ _ _ _ _ _ _ _ architectural support
D. _ _ _ _ _ _ _ fastened with wire
E. _ _ _ _ _ _ parts of a flower
F. _ _ _ _ _ fall from rectitude
G. _ _ _ _ burst of thunder
H. _ _ _ take in with the tongue
I. _ _ father
J. _ article

15. Which triangle below will not fit into the design on the left?

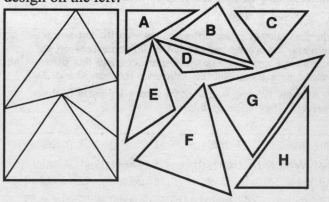

NOW CHECK YOUR ANSWERS
AND KEEP A NOTE OF YOUR SCORE.

Answers

1. 10 (**Score 1 point**)

The last number (represented by X) is double the first number; the penultimate number is double the second number; this pattern is continued throughout.

2. (**Score 1 point if all correct**) A is false (the angle is 165 degrees or 195 degrees); B is true; C is true; D is true (AEFHIKLMNTVWXYZ. Did you refer back to Question 3 in Test 3 in the previous group?)

3. 585 (**Score 1 point**)

The highest and lowest numbers divisible by 13 are 143 and 39 respectively. 91 is midway between them. 91 x 8 = 728; 728 – 143 = 585.

4. K (**Score 1 point**)

It has no counterpart and should be as B, E and O.

5. FOUR 1. SOUR 2. SOUS 3. SONS 4. SINS 5. SINE 6. NINE (**Score 1 point. You may score 1 point if you have used other words as long as they are genuine words.**)

6. 10 (**Score 1 point**)

The first number is the difference between the last two numbers, the second number is the difference between the penultimate and antepenultimate numbers, and this pattern follows throughout. X is the difference between 30 and 20.

7. A scores 195 and B scores 203 (**Score 1 point if both correct**). They score as follows:

A		B	
20 (single)	9 (treble 3)	1 (single)	57 (treble 19)
36 (double 18)	7 (single)	8 (double 4)	16 (single)
39 (treble 13)	16 (double 8)	18 (treble 6)	22 (double 11)
10 (single)	42 (treble 14)	15 (single)	27 (treble 9)
4 (double 2)	12 (single)	34 (double 17)	5 (single)
195		**203**	

8. I IMAGINE I'M A GENUINE GENIUS IN MINING (Score 1 point)

The zodiac sign is obviously GEMINI because the fourth and sixth letters are the same. Substituting the known letters for symbols gives

I IM-GINE IM – GEN-INE GENI-- IN MINING

The missing letter in the fifth word must be U, as GENUINE is the only word that will fit, so the next word must have U as its fifth letter, and the last letter therefore must be S, as GENIUS is the only letter that will fit. The single letter for the fourth word must be A, which is also the only letter that will complete the second word, IMAGINE.

9. (Score 2 points if all correct; score 1 point if 8 correct)

A. GRAFFITO, B. TYMPANI, C. CONCERTO, D. TEMPI, E. PHENOMENON, F. CHARISMATA, G. LOCI, H. LIRE, I. RADII.

10. 6, 1, 14, 14, 20 (Score 1 point)

Give the consonants their alphabetical value omitting vowels. Thus, for example, –BCD–FGH (H is 6). Give the vowels the values A is 1, E is 2, I is 3, O is 4, U is 5.

11. BOW (Score 1 point)

Substitute numbers for letters according to their alphabetical order and then total the numbers in each word: FAIRY (59) matches with WOOF (59) and BUBBLE (44) matches with BESIDE (44). TABLE totals 40, and the only one of the words listed that totals 40 is BOW.

12. F (Score 1 point)

The black bar has been moved further out from the circle.

13. 12 (Score 1 point)

There are two series. Starting with the first term and taking each alternate term thereafter – 7, 9, 12, 16, 21 – the numbers increase by 2, 3, 4 and 5.

Starting with the second term and taking each alternate term thereafter – 3, 7, (12), 18, 25 – the numbers increase by 4, 5, 6 and 7.

14. A. Splattered, B. Plastered, C. Pedestal, D. Stapled,
E. Petals, F. Lapse, G. Peal, H. Lap, I. Pa, J. A **(Score 1 point)**

15. B **(Score 1 point)**

REMEMBER TO KEEP A NOTE OF YOUR SCORE.

Notes: A pretty tough test resulting in generally low scores, although a generous time limit was given. The numerical sequences in Questions 1, 6 and 13 may have puzzled you because of your over-emphasis on numerical ideas at the expense of deduction. Breaking the code in Question 8 would have become surprisingly easy once it was seen that the zodiac sign had to be Gemini.

Questions 10 and 11 prompt me to point out that whenever you meet numbers interspersed with letters you should suspect that the alphabetical order of the letters should be considered, so that numbers can be substituted for letters, although in Question 10 this would have only given you a starting point from which deduction would be called for.

Correctly choosing any one word (especially one of the longer ones) in Question 14 may well have helped you to arrive at the previous or following word.

Test 2

Time limit: 60 minutes
**You may rest after 30 minutes and then
resume for another 30 minutes.**

1. In these unfinished games of noughts and crosses A plays crosses and B plays noughts throughout, and they take turns to start, beginning with A. How many games should each win, and which game is wrong?

```
X | O | X        O | X | O        O |   | O
---------        ---------        ---------
O | X | X          | O | X        O | X | X
---------        ---------        ---------
O |   | O        X | O | X          |   | X
        A                B                C


  O | O | X          | O | X
  ---------        ---------
  X | O | O          |   | X
  ---------        ---------
    | X | X        O |   | X
          D                E


O | X | X          | O | X        X | O | X
---------        ---------        ---------
  | X |            |   | X        X | O | O
---------        ---------        ---------
O | O | X        O |   | X          | X | O
        F                G                H


  O | X | O        X |   | O
  ---------        ---------
  O | X | X          | O | O
  ---------        ---------
  X | O |          X |   | X
          I                J
```

63

2. If September – December is 32 and
May – August is 17, what is January – April?

3. Change PITY into LOVE in six moves and then
change LOVE into FURY in six moves, changing
one letter at a time and making genuine words
each time.

```
    P I T Y        L O V E
1. _ _ _ _     1. _ _ _ _
2. _ _ _ _     2. _ _ _ _
3. _ _ _ _     3. _ _ _ _
4. _ _ _ _     4. _ _ _ _
5. _ _ _ _     5. _ _ _ _
6. L O V E     6. F U R Y
```

4. What is X?

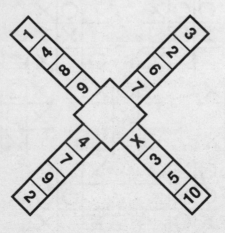

5. Copy this grid and insert words chosen from the list below so that there are words reading across and down

AXLE FLAT
DOFF ANTE
TEAT FETE
DATA OXEN

6. What is X?

6 4 18 14 X 16 30 15 32 1 28 9 8 3

7.

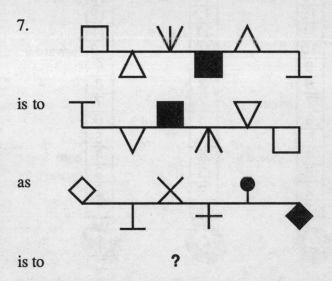

is to

as

is to   ?

8. The counters are moved according to the throw of the die. The throws of the die are as follows 4, 2, 6, 1, 2, 4. Which will be the first counter to reach 21?

A

21	
20	
19	
18	back 3
17	
16	forward 5
15	
14	back 3
13	forward 6
12	
11	
10	
9	
8	
7	back 1
6	
5	
4	forward 6
3	
2	
1	

B

21	
20	forward 1
19	back 4
18	
17	
16	
15	forward 2
14	
13	back 5
12	
11	back 2
10	
9	
8	
7	
6	forward 3
5	
4	
3	
2	
1	

C

21	
20	back 1
19	
18	
17	
16	forward 3
15	
14	
13	back 6
12	
11	
10	forward 5
9	
8	
7	
6	
5	
4	back 3
3	forward 6
2	
1	

9. How many five-letter words can you make out of PALSE?

10.
If 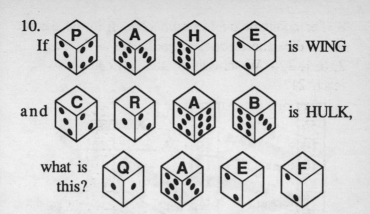 is WING

and is HULK,

what is
this?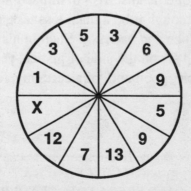

11. Which is the odd one out?
    A. DECODE
    B. SUPERCHARGED
    C. TRAMCAR
    D. WHEELWRIGHT
    E. INSOLENT
    F. CRAYON

12. What is X?

Wheel segments (clockwise from top): 5, 3, 6, 9, 5, 9, 13, 7, 12, X, 1, 3

13. What is this well-known adage from which all the consonants have been removed?

O–E – –A– –O– –OE– –'– –A–E A –U– –E–

14. Arrange these into three pairs.

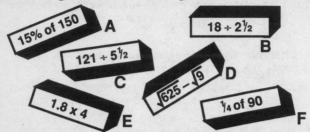

15. A word may be 'concealed' in a sentence. For example, 'I'm omni*scient if I c*laim to know everything,' conceals the word SCIENTIFIC. How many parts of the body can you find in the following?

'A popular man teaches truth to each and everyone; is unselfish in himself and is kind to all, even though it be a thankless task, needing tolerance and patience. Each in his own way should err on the side of justice, yet remain equable, good and, of a certainty, fair in every way.'

NOW CHECK YOUR ANSWERS
AND KEEP A NOTE OF YOUR SCORE.

Answers

1. A should win 2 games; B should win 2 games; game F is wrong. **(Score 1 point if all correct)**

A should win games E and G; B should win games C and J. Game F is wrong because although nought went first there are only three noughts compared with four crosses.

2. 25 **(Score 1 point)**

Add the number of letters in the months: January – 7, February – 8, March – 5 and April – 5 gives a total of 25.

3. (Score 1 point if all correct. You may score 1 point if you have used other words as long as they are genuine words.)

PITY, 1. CITY, 2. CITE, 3. MITE, 4. MOTE, 5. MOVE, 6. LOVE, 1. LORE, 2. LURE, 3. CURE, 4. CURS, 5. FURS, 6. FURY

4. 8 **(Score 1 point)**

Start at 1 and move clockwise. Then consider the second section in the next vane, followed by the third section in the next vane and finally the fourth section in the next vane: 1, 2, 3, 4. Now start at 3 in the second vane (at the top) and move downwards through successive vanes: 3, 5, 7, 9. Next start at 10 in the third vane (at the top) and move in the same way: 10, 9, 8, 7. Finally, start at 2 in the remaining vane (at the top) and move in the same way: 2, 4, 6, (8).

5. (Score 1 point)

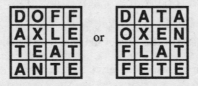

6. 2 **(Score 1 point)**

The first term doubles the last term; the second term halves the penultimate term; the third term doubles the next to last; and so on. Therefore, X must double 1.

7. (Score 1 point)

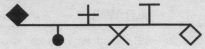

Transpose the symbols in the same way as in the example. (This is in fact only a matter of reversing the order of the symbols and placing them on the opposite side of the central line.)

8. A (Score 1 point)

They move as follows:

	Counter A	Counter B	Counter C
1st move	10	4	1
2nd move	12	9	9
3rd move	15	17	15
4th move	21	18	19
5th move	-	21	21

9. 6 (Score 1 point if all correct)

The words are Lapse, Pales, Peals, Sepal, Pleas and Leaps.

10. Sigh (Score 1 point)

Add the number of spots on each die to the letter shown. For example, Q plus 2 is S.

11. C (Score 1 point)

All the others contain fishes: A. COD, B. PERCH and CHAR, D. EEL, E. SOLE, F. RAY.

12. 17 (Score 1 point)

Starting at 1, moving clockwise and missing two segments each time gives 1, 3, 5, 7. Starting at the next number, 3, and moving in the same way gives 3, 6, 9, 12. Starting at the next number, 5, and moving in the same way gives 5, 9, 13, (17).

13. ONE SWALLOW DOESN'T MAKE A SUMMER (Score 1 point)

14. A–F (each is 22.5), B–E (each is 7.2), C–D (each is 22) **(Score 1 point if all correct)**

15. 11 (Score 2 points if all correct: score 1 point if 9 or 10 correct)

The hidden words are: arm, chest, hand, shin, ankle, knee, chin, shoulder, eye, leg, face.

They are concealed as follows: 'A popular man teaches truth to each and everyone; is unselfish in himself and is kind to all, even though it be a thankless task, needing tolerance and patience. Each in his own way should err on the side of justice, yet remain equable, good, and, of a certainty, fair in every way.'

REMEMBER TO KEEP A NOTE OF YOUR SCORE.

Notes: There were no great difficulties in most of these problems, although Question 15 took a fair amount of time and many of the 'hidden' words were elusive. The time limit allowed for the difficulty of Questions 3, 10, 14 and 15. In Question 13 the apostrophe in 'doesn't' may have led you to the solution.

Test 3

1. Pair the words or parts of words in the first column with those in the second column.

A. HAND	1. LED
B. MIS	2. NAL
C. STOCK	3. TON
D. CAR	4. ADE
E. PAR	5. SHY
F. TEN	6. TAKING
G. EX	7. RIAGE
H. PRO	8. DON
I. MAR	9. ANT
J. FI	10. CESS

2. The first three horses in a race were

1. WINDOW BOX
2. I'M LUCKY ONE
3. OLD QUEEN ANNE

Which of those below came fourth?

A. GENTLEMAN JIM
B. ITALIAN DREAMS
C. INTELLIGENCE TEST
D. NOT QUITE THERE

3. Which of the designs below – A, B, C or D – follows number 6?

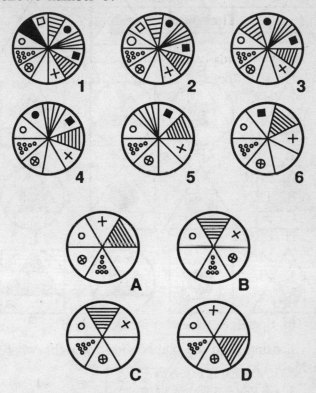

4. Using only plus or minus signs, arrange the numbers below so that they will equal 10. You must use **all** the numbers.

3 4 5 6 7 8 9

5. Which is the odd one out?

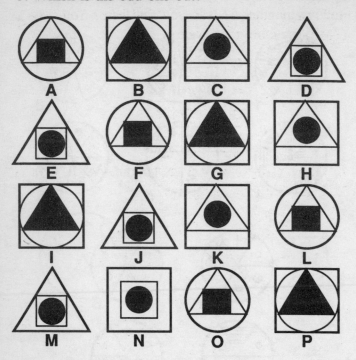

6. Choosing from the numbers on the right, what is X?

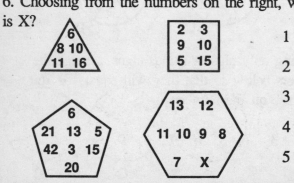

1

2

3

4

5

7. Reading vertically, horizontally or diagonally, how many countries can you find here? You may use letters more than once.

C	A	D	I
H	N	A	L
G	I	T	Y
E	R	I	A

8. Which of the clocks at the bottom – A, B, C or D – should follow number 5?

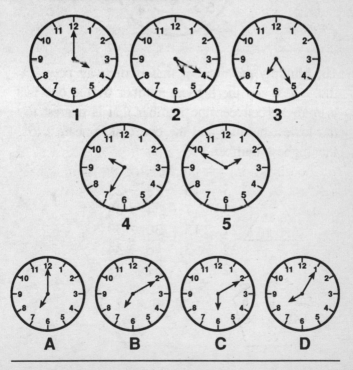

1 2 3

4 5

A B C D

9. What is X?

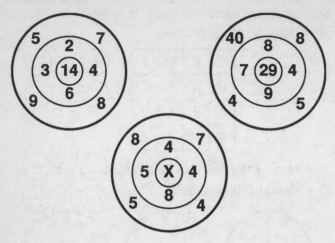

10. Multiply the number that is midway between the lowest and the highest number by the one that is midway between the number that is nearest to the lowest number and the one that is nearest to the highest number.

5	16	28	23
19	7	4	38
21	15	30	39
22	3	6	34
12	25	37	8

11. Which of the shapes below – A, B or C – follows those above?

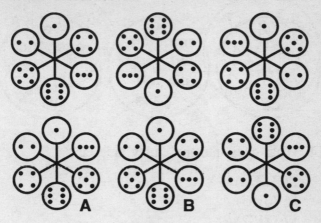

12. Which of the words listed below follows those at the top?

> INTELLIGENCE
> LIABLE
> ABDICATE
> ICONOCLAST
> OCCULT
> CUCUMBER
> UMBRELLA

RIDGE   RIDDLE   EDGE   IDLE   REIGN

13. Use a word or part of a word from each circle to make eight new words.

14. What goes into the empty brackets?

31 (1324)
16 (6183) 42
17 (7132) 38
47 (   ) 23
31 (1376) 48
58 (8542) 67

15. Which is the odd one out?

A. TEN
B. FLY
C. YAK
D. THE
E. NET

Answers

1. A–1, B–6, C–4, D–7, E–8, F–9, G–10, H–3, I–5, J–2 (Score 2 points if all correct; score 1 point if 8 correct)

2. B (Score 1 point)

Give the letters values according to their positions in the alphabet and total all the words in each horse: WINDOW BOX – 129, I'M LUCKY ONE – 128, OLD QUEEN ANNE – 127. The letters in ITALIAN DREAMS give a total of 126.

3. C (Score 1 point)

Beginning with the segment containing ◯ at approximately 10 o'clock in number 1, move clockwise. The segment next to it is removed in number 2 and in each subsequent figure. The number of segments in the circles decreases by one each time, so that from the initial 12 segments, the final circle contains only 6 segments.

4. Because only plus and minus signs are used there are many possible arrangements of these numbers (Score 1 point)

Four examples are:

3+8-7+6-5+9-4

8-6-7+5+9+4-3

4-3+9+8+5-7-6

9-5+6-7+8+3-4

Any permutation of the numbers shown above (with appropriate signs) would have satisfied the question. Of course, if division or multiplication had been required, the number of possible answers would have been very limited.

5. N (Score 1 point)

In no other figure is there a square within a square.

6. 2 (Score 1 point)

The total of the numbers in the triangle (3 sides), 51, is divisible by 3; in the square (4 sides), 44 is divisible by 4; in the pentagon (5 sides), 125 is divisible by 5. Therefore, in the hexagon (6 sides), the total of the numbers must be divisible by 6. As the present numbers total 70, 2 must be added to make 72. Of the numbers offered, only 2 will bring the total to a number divisible by 6.

7. 5 (Score 1 point if all correct)

Canada, Italy, China, Nigeria, India.

8. B (Score 1 point)

The minute hand moves to where the hour hand was in the previous clock; the hour hand advances first one hour, then two hours, then three and so on. After number 5 the hour hand must advance five hours (to 7).

9. 3 (Score 1 point)

Subtract the total of the numbers in the inner ring from the total of the numbers in the outer ring. In the third circle the outer ring totals 24 and the inner ring 21.

10. 441 (Score 1 point)

The lowest number is 3 and the highest number is 39, so the midway number is 21. The number nearest to the lowest number is 4 and the number nearest to the highest number is 38, so the midway number is 21 again. 21 multiplied by 21 is 441.

11. C (Score 1 point)

The top and bottom circles change place each time; the other circles move clockwise throughout.

12. REIGN (Score 1 point)

Each word starts with the middle two letters in the previous word, so the last word must begin with RE, the middle two letters in umbRElla.

13. ecc-en-tric, sa-lv-age, si-mm-er, err-a-tic, in-ver-sion, im-pass-ive, cal-en-dar, cr-usa-der (**Score 1 point if all correct**)

14. 7484 (Score 1 point)

The first two numbers inside the brackets reverse the number on the left outside the brackets. The next two numbers inside the brackets reverse the number on the right outside the brackets in the next line.

15. B (Score 1 point)

Count the number of straight strokes in each word. Those in A, C, D and E each total nine, but there are only eight straight strokes in FLY.

REMEMBER TO KEEP A NOTE OF YOUR SCORE.

Notes: Question 2 called for deduction and would have taken some time to solve and involved much paper work. The spatial problems in Questions 3, 5 and 11 should not have been too difficult, although Question 8 was more difficult. In Question 7 India was the most elusive of the countries among those pre-tested. Question 10 could have been worked out mentally, but almost certainly required paper work and took some time, although it was not generally considered as difficult as the previous test

Test 4

Time limit: 45 minutes

1. What goes into the empty segment?

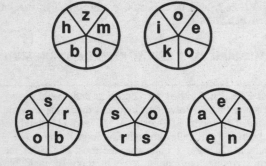

2.

$$\frac{Z+T+Q+I}{G+K} = D \quad \text{what is} \quad W+Q+J-N?$$

If

Choose from: K+Y   X+L+F   V+M   V+H+D

3. Find the two famous composers who are scrambled in each of these phrases.

    A. GRANDER VIEW
    B. BIG CHARGE
    C. HE BOASTS VENTURES

4. Which is the odd one out?

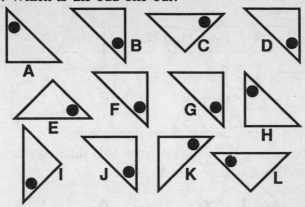

5. What goes into the bottom square?

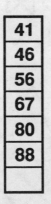

41
46
56
67
80
88

6. How many cubes can you count here?

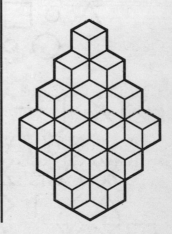

7. Which is the odd one out?

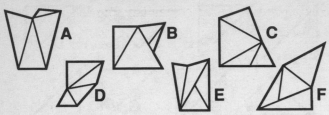

8. If you can decode these five months successfully you should have little difficulty in decoding the statement below.

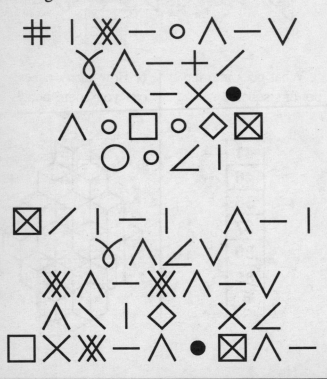

9. Which two pieces will fit with the piece above to complete a square containing four-letter words across and down?

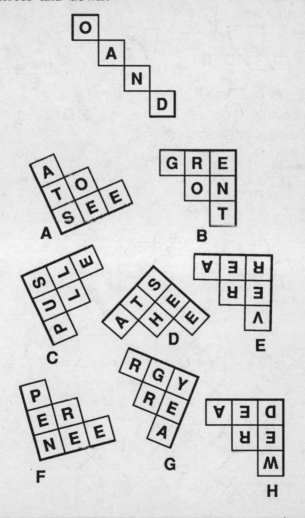

A

B

C

D

E

F

G

H

10. There are five groups of teeth here, with four identical sets in each group. Match the five groups and state which teeth will not mesh with any of the other sets.

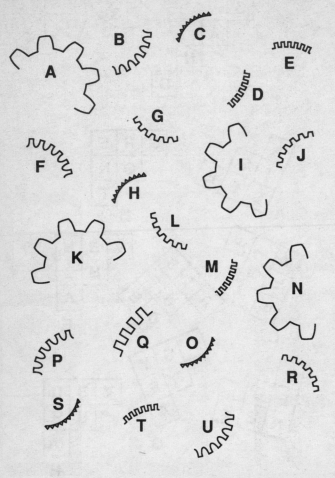

11. What are X and Y?

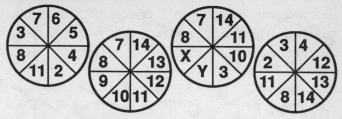

12. If PEREGRINATION = 44 and
        AFFECTIONATE = 36 and
    MISAPPREHENSION = 44
what is COMMONPLACE?

13. Which one is wrong?

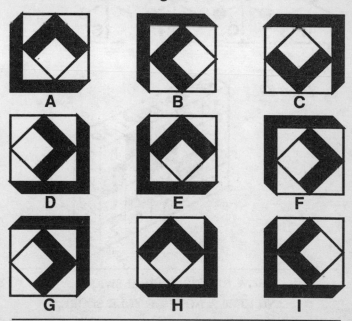

A   B   C

D   E   F

G   H   I

14. Which two make a pair?

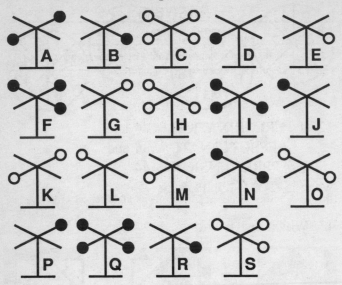

15. What are X, Y and Z?

**NOW CHECK YOUR ANSWERS
AND KEEP A NOTE OF YOUR SCORE.**

Answers

1. P (Score 1 point)

Take each letter in turn from the first circle, advancing one segment in each of the subsequent circles.

$$Z\ E\ B\ R\ A$$
$$M\ O\ O\ S\ E$$
$$O\ K\ A\ \underline{P}\ I$$
$$B\ I\ S\ O\ N$$
$$H\ O\ R\ S\ E$$

2. K+Y (Score 1 point)

Give each letter a value according to its alphabetical order:

$$\frac{26+20+17+9}{7+11} = \frac{72}{18} = 4\ (D)$$

$$23+17+10 = 50 - 14\ (N) = 36$$

The only combination of letters at the bottom that totals 36 is K+Y (24+12).

3. A. VERDI and WAGNER, B. BACH and GRIEG, C. BEETHOVEN and STRAUSS (Score 1 point if all correct)

4. C (Score 1 point)

The spot is on the right of the right angle; in all the others it is on the left.

5. 104 (Score 1 point)

Each number is the sum of the digits in the previous number added to the previous number; 88+16=104.

6. 24 **(Score 1 point)**

When viewed from above there are 15 cubes; a further 9 can be seen when they are viewed from underneath. These nine can be seen more clearly if you focus your attention on the cubes with white bases and black side faces emphasized here.

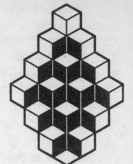

(Although the structure was made up with 15 cubes, the question was 'how many can you **count**?')

7. A **(Score 1 point)**

In A there are two right-angled triangles, one isosceles triangle and one scalene triangle. In all the others there are: one right-angled triangle, one equilateral triangle, one isosceles triangle and one scalene triangle.

8. There are many Barbary apes in Gibraltar **(Score 1 point)**

The five months depicted in code are February, March, April, August and June. Once these were solved, there remained little difficulty in breaking the coded statement.

9. C and H **(Score 1 point if both correct)**

They fit together like this

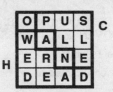

10. A–I–K–N, B–F–P–U, C–H–O–S, D–E–M–T, G–J–L–R **(Score 1 point if all correct)**

Q will not mesh with any of the other teeth.

11. X is 10 and Y is 9 **(Score 1 point if both correct)**

Consider the same segments that are occupied by X and Y in the other circles:

8	9	10(X)	11
11	10	9(Y)	8

12. 36 (Score 1 point)

Add the value of the vowels from their positions in the alphabet: A = 1, E = 5, I = 9 and O = 15.

13. F (Score 1 point)

The black sides of the centre square rotate anti-clockwise; the black sides of the outer square rotate clockwise. In F the black sides of the centre square have rotated clockwise.

14. B and R (Score 1 point)

15. X is 12, Y is 0 and Z is 3 (Score 1 point)

By elimination ■ must be 2 and can be substituted where it occurs elsewhere. In the third horizontal row ● must be 6 (so that row adds to 29).

REMEMBER TO KEEP A NOTE OF YOUR SCORE.

Notes: The easiest questions of this group. Even the decoding in Question 8 presented little difficulty; slightly more difficult than the decoding of the statement was the decoding of the months, although the number of letters contained in them was of assistance, as was also, for example, the repetition of U in August. Question 15 was probably the most difficult.

Overall scoring in this test was higher, although restricted somewhat by the shorter time limit, which was deliberately imposed.

NOW TOTAL YOUR SCORES FOR THE FOUR TESTS IN THIS GROUP AND COMPARE THEM WITH THE RATINGS THAT FOLLOW.

Ratings in Group II

Test 1 – average 7 points
Test 2 – average 6 points
Test 3 – average 7 points
Test 4 – average 8 points

Total for the group out of a possible 63 points

Over 50	Excellent
40–50	Very good
29–39	Good
28	Average
22–27	Fair
Under 22	Poor

The tests will now become more difficult, so if you had a very low rating in this group I suggest that before you go on to Group III you start from the beginning and go carefully through all the problems again, trying to understand the reasoning behind the answers and explanations.

GROUP III
– Difficult –

Test 1

Time limit: 1 hour
**You may rest after 30 minutes and then
resume for a further 30 minutes.**

1. If   FIVE+TWENTY = TWENTY-FIVE
                TWELVE = TWENTY
          NINE+TEN = FIFTEEN

What is TWENTY-FIVE–TWELVE?

Choose one of these:

FIVE TEN THIRTEEN FIFTY NINE ELEVEN

2. Which is the odd one out?

   A. BARBICAN
   B. CADRE
   C. ALUMINIUM
   D. TREMENDOUS
   E. INDEFENSIBLE

3. Copy this grid and complete the puzzle from the words listed.

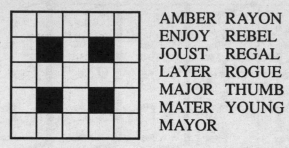

AMBER RAYON
ENJOY REBEL
JOUST REGAL
LAYER ROGUE
MAJOR THUMB
MATER YOUNG
MAYOR

4. Group these illustrations into one set of five, two sets of three and one pair and state which is the odd one out.

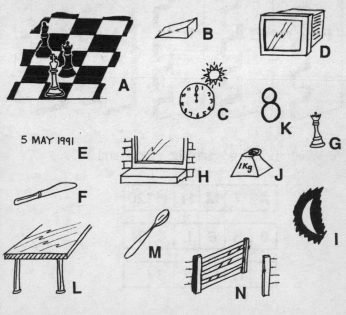

5. Which of these prevents a perfect fit? Is it a mortise or tenon?

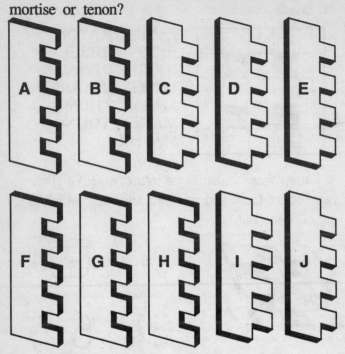

6. What should go into the empty square?

A	7	M	11	H	20

9	H	6	L	4	N

1	G	13	K	8	

7. Alf earns £110 per week and has been promised a rise of 10 per cent next year and 7 per cent the following year. Bert earns £120 per week and has been promised a rise of 5 per cent next year and 4 per cent the following year. Charlie earns £125 per week and has been promised a rise of 3 per cent next year and 2 per cent the following year. At the end of the two years who will be earning the highest weekly wage and what will be the differential between the lowest and highest paid?

8. Make eight pairs out of these pictures. Which is the odd one out?

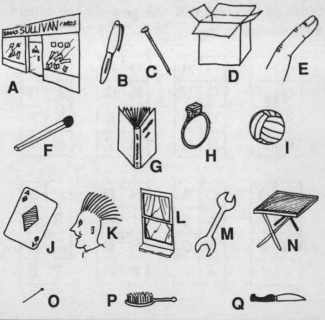

9. If this card

were turned round (so that the bottom became the top and vice versa) it would look quite different:

If all the picture cards are removed from a normal pack of cards there will be 40 cards left. How many cards of that 40 would look different if they were turned round as in the example above?

10. There are eight eight-letter words hidden in these figures. Start by finding the word WARDROBE, and that will give you the pattern for the other words.

W	B
C	C
A	C
C	O

R	A
O	U
U	R
U	R

O	N
R	O
R	S
M	P

B	C
A	D
K	T
H	C

H	O
K	M
R	C
A	I

O	A
A	E
E	O
A	I

N	N
I	R
R	N
B	S

E	S
S	R
D	Y
T	E

11. What do these dates have in common?
    15 February 1984
    2 July 1983
    16 December 1983

12. What is X?

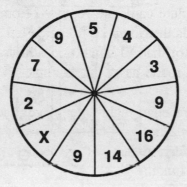

13. Add all the square numbers to their relative square roots and subtract the sum of the numbers remaining.

25	5	2	82	11
98	440	64	537	302
1225	35	15	225	7
19	4	9	3	8

14. What word do the three cards at the bottom represent?

= WIT

= MUG

= ?

15. Lucie, Mary, Ann, Lily, Jenny, Jim, George, Bert, Tom and Fred sat on the two long sides of a

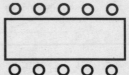

rectangular table the ladies alternating with, and sitting opposite to, the men.

Fred sat in a centre position. Lily sat opposite George. Mary sat next to Fred and three places from George. Jenny sat four places to the left of Lily. Ann sat two places from Mary. Tom sat opposite Mary. Bert sat three places from Jenny. Copy the rectangle and indicate where everyone sat.

**NOW CHECK YOUR ANSWERS
AND KEEP A NOTE OF YOUR SCORE.**

Answers

1. FIVE (Score 1 point)

Add the number of straight strokes that make up the words:

FIVE (10) plus TWENTY (18) = 28

TWENTY-FIVE = 28

TWELVE = 18

TWENTY = 18

The only word at the bottom that contains 10 strokes (the difference between 28 and 18) is FIVE.

2. E (Score 1 point)

All the other words contain three consecutive letters of the alphabet spaced alternately: A. bArBiCan, B. CaDrE, C. aLuMiNium, D. treMeNdOus.

INDEFENSIBLE contains three consecutive letters of the alphabet following each other.

3. (Score 1 point)

4. A–E–J–K–N, B–H–L, C–I–M, D–G. F is the odd one out. **(Score 1 point if all correct)**

These are rhyming groups: A–mate (The white king is in checkmate to the black queen and bishop), E–date, J–weight, K–eight, N–gate; B–wedge, H–ledge, L–edge; C–noon (It cannot be midnight as the sun is shining), I–moon, M–spoon; D–screen, G–queen. Nothing rhymes with knife (F).

5. I; it is a tenon **(Score 1 point if both correct)**

A, B, F, G and H are all mortises (cavities to receive tenons); C, D, E, I and J are all tenons. The projections on I are too long.

6. T (Score 1 point)

In the bottom row numbers are substituted for letters (or letters for numbers) compared with the top row. T (the 20th letter) corresponds with 20 in the top row. (The middle row has no bearing on this comparison and is merely a 'red herring'.)

7. Charlie and £1.85 (Score 1 point if both correct)

Alf's weekly wage will be £129.47; Bert's weekly wage will be £131.04; Charlie's weekly wage will be £131.32. The difference between Alf's and Charlie's wages is £1.85.

8. B–Q(pen knife), E–C (finger nail), G–A (book shop), H–M (ring spanner), I–F (football match), K–P (hair brush), O–N (pin table), L–D (window box). The playing card (J) is the odd one out **(Score 1 point if all correct)**

9. 22 (Score 1 point)

The cards that would look different are

♥	♣	♦	♠
Ace	Ace		Ace
3	3		3
5	5		5
6	6		6
7	7	7	7
8	8		8
9	9		9

10. Wardrobe, Bookcase, Curtains, Cushions, Armchair, Cupboard, Crockery, Ornament **(Score 1 point if all correct)**

The pattern followed throughout can be seen by noting how the first two words are obtained.

11. They all fall in the middle **(Score 1 point)**

15 February was the middle of February (1984 being a leap year); 2 July was the middle day of the year 1983; and 16 December was the middle of December.

12. 7 (Score 1 point)

The numbers in the lower half are the sum of the two numbers in the opposite upper half (2+7=9; 7+9=16; 9+5=14; 5+4=9. Hence 4+3=7(X).)

13. 124 (Score 1 point)

The sum of the square numbers and their relative square roots –
25, 5, 64, 8, 1225, 35, 15, 225, 4, 2, 9 and 3 – is 1620. The sum
of 82, 11, 98, 440, 537, 302, 7 and 19 is 1496. 1620 less 1496
equals 124.

14. LIT (Score 1 point)

The 13 cards in each of the two suits at the top indicate the 26
letters of the alphabet, but read backwards. Thus hearts represent
M – A from the Ace upwards and diamonds represent Z – N
from the Ace upwards. In the bottom row, therefore, 2 of hearts
is L, 5 of hearts is I (see also top row) and 7 of diamonds is T
(see also top row).

15. (Score 1 point)   **Jim Mary Fred Ann George**

Jenny Tom Lucie Bert Lily

REMEMBER TO KEEP A NOTE OF YOUR SCORE.

Notes: A very difficult test and extremely low scores were
the norm as the time limit was deliberately imposed to
encourage quick working, especially as much numerical
writing was necessary. Although the actual time involved in
writing was allowed for, no concession was made for slow
solving.

Many would have been caught out by the pictorial
representations in Question 8; if, for example, 'shop' was
paired with 'window', or 'ring' with 'finger' – or even with
'diamond' – further pairing would have been impossible.
The number of playing cards that appear differently when
turned round caught everyone out in extensive pre-testing.

All in all, your brain must have been reeling after tackling
this test!

Test 2

1. What is X?

2. Which of these statements are true and which are false?

  A. When the time is either 5.50 or 10.30 the hands of a clock form an angle of 120 degrees.

  B. London is further south than Newfoundland.

  C. Greenland is the largest island in the world.

3. What numbers do the letters represent? The first calculation is an addition; the second is a subtraction.

	A B C		A B C
	D E F		D E F
	1 2 1 6		2 5 4

4. What is the total of the numbers in the cross?

1	5	9	0	8	6	7	1
4	2	8	7	5	6	2	0
1	6	3	8	9	3	5	6
1	2	8		4	7	6	5
0	7				1	9	8
5	8	6		0	6	7	5
6	7	0	1	5	9	7	8
8	6	9	5	7	6	0	8

5. A man has a certain number of cigarettes and resolves to give up smoking when they are all gone. He decides to smoke one cigarette each morning, then to destroy half of those remaining, and to smoke one at night. After four days he has none left. How many cigarettes did he have to start with?

6. Which, if any, of these are wrong?

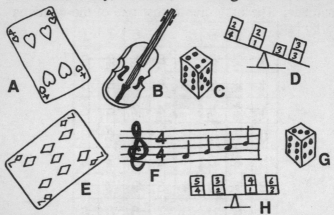

7. Which of the numbered cubes on the right belong in the spaces A, B, C and D?

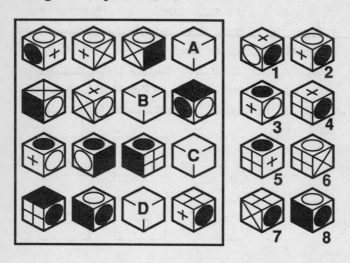

8. Copy this grid and substitute letters for numbers. The only clue is that one of the words is WRITHED.

1	2	3	3	2	3	4
2		5		6		7
4	6	8	9	6	10	11
4		6		2		8
10	12	13	14	15	10	4
4		10		16		6
4	8	11	8	9	17	4

9. How many combinations of three of these numbers will add to 100?

32	39	34	27
35	33	29	31
28	40	38	41

10. Two couples played each other at darts: A and B played together and C and D were partners. They used the dartboard shown below, on which the bull scores 50. Player A scored all numbers divisible by 4, plus the bull; player B scored all numbers divisible by 3, plus the bull; player C scored all numbers divisible by 7, plus the bull; and player D scored all even numbers, excluding the bull.

Which team won, and what were the individual scores?

11. Which is the odd one out and why?

A. MOLLY
B. CELIA
C. MYRA
D. RONALD
E. CORAL
F. ROLAND
G. AMY
H. ARNOLD

12. From the two seasons shown here in code you must decode two messages.

The messages are an announcement from a tone-deaf artiste taking part in a concert and the opening words of a letter from a veracious correspondent.

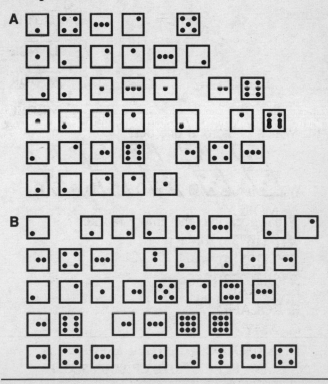

13. Find the words that will link the previous word with the following word throughout the sequence. For example:
test (MATCH) box.

BABY
A _____
STAND
B _____
DREAM
C _____
LORD
D _____
YARD
E _____
CHAIR
F _____
DATE
G _____
DUTY
H _____
LANCE
I _____
MAJOR
J _____
MODEL

14. Which is the odd one out?

15. What goes into the empty brackets?
441 (14736) 144
625 (12516) 96
756 (10832) 256
108 (   ) 90

**NOW CHECK YOUR ANSWERS
AND KEEP A NOTE OF YOUR SCORE.**

Answers

1. F (Score 1 point)

Consider the four numbers in the four opposite segments. Subtract the sum of the two lowest numbers from that of the two highest numbers. The letter derives from the alphabetical position of the result.

2. A. False, B. False, C. True (Score 1 point if all correct)

In A note that the hour hand will not be exactly on the hour.

3. A is 7, B is 3, C is 5, D is 4, E is 8 and F is 1 (Score 1 point if all correct)

```
  7 3 5      7 3 5
  4 8 1      4 8 1
 ───────    ───────
1 2 1 6      2 5 4
```

4. 21 (Score 1 point)

Follow arithmetical progressions diagonally. Start at the top left-hand corner: 1, 2, 3, 4, 5, 6, 7, 8. Start at the top right-hand corner: 1, 2, 3, 4, 5, 6, 7, 8. Start at the third number down on the left-hand side: 1, 2, 3, 4, 5, 6. The cross is filled thus

```
      4
  3   5   5
      4
```

5. 45 (Score 1 point)

	Start	Smoked	Destroyed	Smoked	Left
1st day	45	1	22	1	21
2nd day	21	1	10	1	9
3rd day	9	1	4	1	3
4th day	3	1	1	1	0

Notice that the number destroyed falls in the progression 22, 10, 4 and 1 (that is, by 12, 6 and 3).

6. B, D, E, F and G (**Score 1 point if all correct**)

In B the sound holes are the wrong way round. In D the balance should go down on the left, as the six-weight on the right is not at the end. In E the central diamond should be off-centre. In F the treble clef is the wrong way round. In G the 4 and 3 spots on the die should be opposite each other.

7. A is 8, B is 3, C is 5, D is 1 (**Score 1 point if all correct**)

In each row the position of either the black spot or the white spot remains the same, and this gives a clear indication of the direction in which the cube is rotating.

8. (**Score 1 point**)

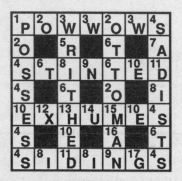

There is only one valid position for WRITHED because all the other words contain the same letter more than once. Now examine the first vertical line. The two identical letters with which it ends must surely be LL or SS but if the former, the last vertical line would finish with TL. The probability of it being S is strengthened by the possible plural endings of at least three of the other words.

The second horizontal line could be 'stilted' or 'stinted', but the last horizontal line obviously favours it being STINTED, so that the last line is SIDINGS.

The last vertical line must be SADISTS, given the letters that have already been placed.

Look at that extraordinary horizontal line at the top. Whether it is 'bow-wows' or 'pow-wows' is not yet clear, but reference to the first vertical line confirms that it is 'pow-wows'. Now look at the third vertical line OTTO_ _N. OTTOMAN will spring to mind immediately, and EXHUMES is the only word to satisfy E_H_MES.

9. 13 (Score 1 point, but only if all correct)

The combinations are:

27	32	41	28	34	38
27	34	39	29	32	39
27	35	38	29	33	38
27	33	40	29	31	40
28	31	41	31	34	35
28	32	40	32	33	35
28	33	39			

10. A and B won (Score 1 point if all correct)

The individual scores were: A – 110 (4–16–8–12–20–50); B – 113 (18–6–15–3–9–12–50); C – 71 (7–14–50); and D – 110 (18–4–6–10–2–16–8–14–12–20).

11. A (Score 1 point)

All the other names are anagrams of other names: Celia (Alice), Myra (Mary), Ronald (Arnold, Roland), Coral (Carol), Roland (Arnold, Ronald), Amy (May), Arnold (Ronald, Roland).

12. A. When a singer rises to sing I go into the wings. B. I write in the first instance to tell the truth. (Score 1 point if both correct)

Although all the seasons have six letters, two - Autumn and Summer - contain the same letter twice, so the two seasons in code must be SPRING and WINTER. As to which is which, the I and N in both words show that the first is Spring and the second is Winter. Armed with this knowledge it is fairly easy to break the codes.

13. A – GRAND, B – PIPE, C – LAND, D – SHIP, E – ARM, F – MAN, G – STAMP, H – FREE, I – SERGEANT, J – SCALE (Score 2 points if all correct; score 1 point if 8 or 9 correct)

14. C (Score 1 point)

It is the only domino that does not have a centre spot.

15. 129 (Score 1 point)

Divide the numbers outside the brackets by 3, 4, 5, 6, 7 and 8. For example, 441 divided by 3 is 147 and 144 divided by 4 is 36. In the last line divide 108 by 9 (12) and 90 by 10 (9).

REMEMBER TO KEEP A NOTE OF YOUR SCORE.

Notes: In the pre-testing no one solved Question 5, although doubtless the time limit beat them. I would recommend that you work backwards. It is immediately apparent that the man must start the last day with three cigarettes, and equally apparent that he must start the third day with nine. Continuing this train of thought, you might have discovered how many cigarettes he started with each day.

In Question 6 you may have not considered the seven of diamonds to be wrong, believing that the diamond in the centre should be as shown. Both Questions 8 and 9 probably occupied you for some time, although ample allowance was made for copying the grid in Question 8. Question 9 required much paper work. Solving the coded messages in Question 12 was not difficult once you decided what the two seasons were.

TEST 3

Time limit: 1 hour
You may rest after 30 minutes and then
continue for a further 30 minutes.

1. Which is the odd one out?

    1   2   B   3   C   5   D   G   8   J   9   P

2. The six faces of a cube are numbered as
follows:

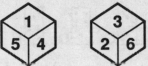

Which of those below is wrong?

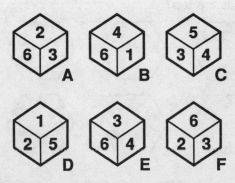

3. Which of the dominoes below – A, B, C, D, E or F – will complete those above?

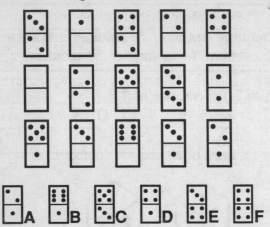

4. Which of the four hexagons at the bottom should occupy the space left by the second hexagon at the top?

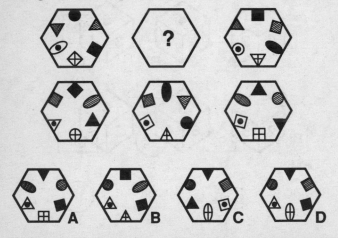

5. Which of the dominoes on the right should be placed at A, B, C and D so that the spots in each row, horizontally and vertically, total 16?

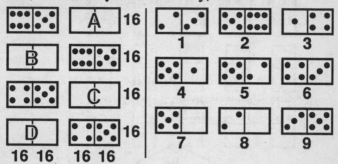

6. What is X?

1 2 4 3 4 8 5 6 12 7 8 16 9 10
20 11 X 24

7. Which is the odd one out?

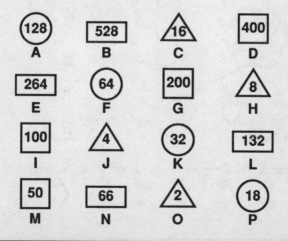

8. A world-famous name is concealed in these sentences:

   CHEATS REALLY ARE IGNOBLE
   CHEAT A PUPIL IN A CITATION

9. Taking a letter first from the top face, then from the left face and finally from the right face, how many three-letter words can you form without using the same square twice?

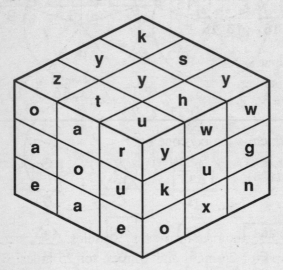

10. What is X?

   1 2 8 4 2 9 4 3 X 2 6 7 4 5 6 1 7 3

11. Avoiding plurals, find the two *different* letters that will make two words in the first circle, one letter that will complete the word in the second circle, four letters that will give four words in the third circle, and the one letter that will complete the last word. From these eight letters how many five-letter words can you form?

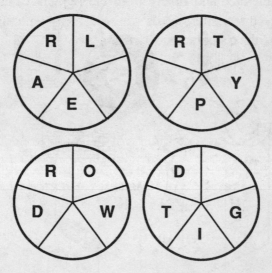

12. Four motorists drove for 50 miles. A averaged 30 mph for 25 miles and 20 mph for 25 miles; B averaged 25 mph throughout; C averaged 20 mph for 15 miles and 35 mph for 35 miles; D averaged 15 mph for 18 miles and 30 mph for 32 miles.

Who did the journey in the shortest time and who took the longest time?

13. Group these illustrations into four sets of three.

A

B

C

D

E

F

G

H
TOM
DICK
HARRY

I

J

K
ARSENAL 1 EVERTON 1

L

14. Which of the figures at the bottom – A, B, C or D – belongs to number 5?

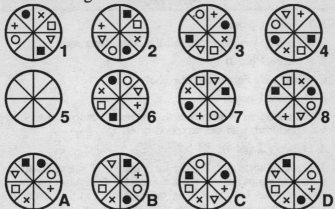

15. What is X?

Answers

1. 1 (Score 1 point)

It is the only straight stroke; all the others have curves.

2. F (Score 1 point)

Compare with right-hand cube above.

3. D (Score 1 point)

All combinations of dominoes that represent numbers from 0 to 6 are included, with the exception of 4/1 (5).

4. D (Score 1 point)

This can be seen by following the sequence of shapes from the third hexagon at the top. All the interior shapes move one place anti-clockwise, but the shading (as established in the first of the top hexagons) *remains in the same position throughout.*

5. A–1, B–3, C–6, D–5 (Score 1 point)

The result is as follows: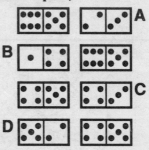

6. 12 (Score 1 point)

There are three series. Starting with the first term and taking every third one thereafter: 1, 3, 5, 7, 9, 11. Starting with the second term and proceeding in the same way: 2, 4, 6, 8, 10, (12) X. Starting with the third term and proceeding in the same way: 4, 8, 12, 16, 20, 24.

7. P (Score 1 point)

The numbers are progressively halved according to the shapes that surround them, so P should be 16 to fit into the sequence 128, 64, 32, 16.

8. CHARLIE CHAPLIN (**Score 1 point**)

Start with the first letter, then take the second letter, then miss one, followed by two, three and so on, as seen below:

<u>CH</u>EATS <u>RE</u>ALLY ARE <u>I</u>GNOBL<u>E</u>

<u>CH</u>E<u>A</u>T A <u>PU</u>PI<u>L</u> IN A <u>C</u>ITATIO<u>N</u>

9. 9 (**Score 1 point**)

It will be found that the same pattern is followed throughout to give zoo, yak, key, tax, you, saw, urn, hug and yew: z (top face bottom left), o (left face top left), o (right face bottom left), y (top face middle left), a (left face middle left), k (right face middle left) and so on.

10. 8 (**Score 1 point**)

The first two numbers equal the last one; the third number is the sum of the two before the last; the sum of the next two (4 and 2) is the fourth from last (6). This pattern is followed throughout.

11. SEPIA, SPINE, SPINY, PANSY, SPAIN (**Score 1 point if you have 4 or 5 correct, as one – Spain – is not a common noun**)

The missing letters in the circles are: P or Y (PEARL or EARLY); A (PARTY); N, S, E or Y (DROWN, SWORD or WORDS, WORDY, ROWED); and I (DIGIT).

12. C took the shortest time, D took the longest time (**Score 1 point if both correct**)

The times taken were: A – 2 hours and 5 minutes, B – 2 hours, C – 1 hour and 45 minutes, D – 2 hours and 16 minutes.

13. A–I–L, B–E–K, C–G–J, D–F–H (**Score 1 point if all correct**)

They are grouped according to the occurrence of the same three consecutive letters in the words: ciGARette (A), GARter (I), ciGAR (L); aCORn (B), reCORd (E), sCORe (K); mALLet (C), bALL (G), wALL (J); cAMEra (D), frAME (F), nAMEs (H).

14. D (**Score 1 point**)

Each segment moves clockwise in alternate circles, missing one segment each time.

15. 0 (Score 1 point)

The totals of the three numbers in opposite segments are halved and doubled alternately. The three numbers opposite X total 20 (7, 9 and 4); therefore, the total of the three numbers in the segment occupied by X must be 10. As the present total is already 10, X must be zero.

REMEMBER TO KEEP A NOTE OF YOUR SCORE.

Notes: Question 8 caused many problems as the hidden letters in the words Charlie Chaplin were so obscured because of the unusual spacing of the letters, which followed the sequence of missing an extra letter each time. Question 9 was not too difficult once it was realized that the same pattern for selecting letters was followed throughout. In Question 13 many people would not have noticed that the letters in the pictures were common to more than one in each group. Question 14 called for lateral thinking, as it is more customary to follow spatial series consecutively rather than alternately, see example on page 11.

NOW TOTAL YOUR SCORES FOR THE THREE TESTS IN THIS GROUP AND COMPARE THEM WITH THE RATINGS THAT FOLLOW.

AFTER THAT, YOU CAN FIND YOUR OVERALL RATING FOR ALL THE TESTS.

Ratings in Group III

Test 1 – average 5 points
Test 2 – average 5 points
Test 3 – average 4 points

Total for the group out of a possible 46 points

Over 30	Excellent
23 – 29	Very good
15 – 22	Good
14	Average
10 – 13	Fair
Under 10	Poor

The tests in this group were extremely tough, and in the pre-testing that was carried out there were many problems that no one managed to solve – or certainly within the given time. In several cases the solutions were eventually arrived at, but only after the time limit had expired. As is always the case, some problems thought relatively easy by some, completely baffled others. 'One man's meat...'

Overall Ratings for All the Tests

The total number of possible points is 169, and the average score throughout is 68.

Group I – 26
Group II – 28
Group II – 14
TOTAL 68

Over 130 Excellent
100 – 130 Very Good
71 – 99 Good
68 – 70 Average
52 – 67 Fair
Under 52 Poor

As mentioned in the Introduction, while a specific IQ factor may apply to one's ability in one particular subject, it does not necessarily indicate what it would be in a variety of subjects. But even the word 'variety' is strictly limited when it is applied to printed word, number or spatial problems of the kind that can be included in a book such as this. A reader may exhibit talent far above the average yet not even attain an average rating in this book. For example, the motor abilities – skills requiring manual dexterity as opposed to mental ability – remain untested by the printed words here.

I trust you regarded these tests primarily as a diversion and feel neither too clever if you had a high rating nor too deflated if your rating was low.